Soho Theatre presents

SHUCK 'N' JIVE

CASSIOPEIA BERKELEY-AGYEPONG
& SIMONE IBBETT-BROWN

Shuck 'n' Jive was first performed
at Soho Theatre on Wednesday 2 October 2019

Cast

Olivia Onyehara	SIMONE
Tanisha Spring	CASSI

Creatives

Cassiopeia Berkeley-Agyepong	Writer/Producer
Simone Ibbett-Brown	Writer/Musical Director
Lakesha Arie-Angelo	Director
Ranya El Refaey	Set and Costume Designer
Jai Morjaria	Lighting Designer
Anna Clock	Sound Designer
Diane Alison-Mitchell	Movement Director
Adam Brace	Associate Director
Nadine Rennie CDG	Casting Director
Ian Taylor	Production Manager
Holly De Angelis	Producer (Soho Theatre)
Grace Lewis	Stage Manager

SIMONE – Olivia Onyehara

Olivia trained at Drama Studio London. Her theatre credits include: *Twelfth Night/Hamlet* (Rose Theatre York); *Jack Lear* (Hull Truck); *A Midsummer Night's Dream/Macbeth* (Rose Theatre York); *Pride and Prejudice* (Nottinhgam Playhouse/ York Theatre Royal); *Private Lives* (Mercury Theatre); *Our American Cousin* (Finborough Theatre); *The Watchers* (Southwark Playhouse); *Twelfth Night* (Iris Theatre); *Time and the Conways* (Nottingham Playhouse); *All Our Daughters?* (New Vic Theatre) and *Tanzi Libre* (Southwark Playhouse). Her screen credits include: *Shallott, My Name is Jo, Drone Strike* and *Casualty*.

CASSI – Tanisha Spring

Theatre credits include: *Prince of Egypt* (Workshop/Dominion Theatre); *Little Shop of Horrors* (Storyhouse); *Making Porn* (Above the Stag); *Caroline or Change* (The Playhouse Theatre); *Big Fish* (The Other Palace); *One Love* (Birmingham Rep); *Beautiful: Carol King Musical* (Aldwych Theatre). TV/Film credits include: *Once an Old Lady...* (Genesis Child Films); *Old Spice She Nose Best*; *Smart Energy UK (*Somesuch); *Baileys Pour Spectacular: League of Their Own* (Sky - Choreographer); *Dancing Queen* (Left Eye Blind - Choreographer). Other Credits: Lights EP - Kitchen Party (Island Records).

Writer/Producer – Cassiopeia Berkeley-Agyepong

Cassiopeia is an actress, singer and theatre-maker passionate about new writing in theatre and opera. Cassi trained at the Royal Academy of Music, having previously studied Music at the University of York. She made her West End debut in *Caroline, or Change*; has assistant directed for ENO Baylis; and is a member of ETT Forge producers' network. Favourite credits and current projects include: Lucy Parsons in *Haymarket* (Actors' Church); *#blessed: a spoken word cabaret* by Martha Pothen (Producer); *CONTAINED* (Writer); *Ophelia* (Composer); *Wonderland - A New Musical* by Olly Wood & Andy Bewley (Producer). @CassiopeiaBA | CassiopeiaBA.com

Writer/Musical Director – Simone Ibbett-Brown

Simone is a theatre-maker, performer and Joint Artistic Director of HERA. HERA celebrates and shares unheard music and stories by equity-seeking artists across the UK. As a theatre-maker, recent work includes directing *Il barbiere di Siviglia* (Devon Opera, tour); *I Capuleti e i Montecchi* (Goodenough College); *Dido and Aeneas* (Leicester MusicFest); and assisting with Glyndebourne, English National Opera and ENO Baylis. As a performer, recent highlights include A Woman in ENO's Olivier Award-winning *Porgy and Bess*; Jo in Palmer & Hall's *Dead Equal* (Summerhall); Esther in *Mamzer Bastard* (workshop, Royal Opera); and Backing Vocals for Mercury Award-winner Benjamin Clementine (European tour). She also performs with protest theatre company, Earth Ensemble. simoneibbettbrown.com

Director – Lakesha Arie-Angelo

Lakesha is Soho Theatre's Associate Director. Work as a Director includes: *Summer Fest* (The Bunker); *soft animals* (Soho Theatre); *The Hoes* (Hampstead Theatre); *Alive Day* (Bunker Theatre) for Pint Sized Plays; *AS:NT* (Theatre503 - as part of Rapid Write); and *Prodigal* (Bush Theatre - for 'Artistic Directors of the Future Black Lives: Black Words'). Work as Assistant Director at Soho includes *The One*; *Touch*; *Blueberry Toast*; and *Roller Diner* (2017 West End Wilma Award for Best Comedy). Work as a playwright includes *Graveyard Gang* for Tamasha Theatre's associate company; *Purple Moon Drama* (Richmix, Poplar Union and community tour). Lakesha's previous work as Resident Assistant Director at the Finborough includes *P'Yongyang*; *Treasure* and *Vibrant 2015 Festival of Finborough Playwrights*. During the residency at the Finborough, Lakesha was awarded the Richard Carne Trust sponsorship.

Set and Costume Designer – Ranya El Refaey

Ranya is a set and costume designer based in London and a graduate from Wimbledon College of Arts. Ranya's artistic passions vary from theatre to fashion to installation art. Since graduating from Wimbledon a year ago, Ranya has worked as a designer and art director in a variety of different fields from music videos, short films, photoshoots and theatre. Her theatrical design credits include: *Stains* (Lyric Hammersmith); *Girl World* (Edinburgh Fringe Festival); *Love songs to Guinea Pigs* (Vaults festival & Soho Theatre); *Black Ice* (Theatre 503); *Love and War* (Lyric Hammersmith); and *The Mob Reformers* (Lyric Hammersmith). Other design credits include *Las Mujeres de Fuego* (Dazed Beauty) and *Working Bitch* (Ashnikko). www.ranyaelrefaey.com

Lighting Designer – Jai Morjara

Jai trained at RADA and won the 2016 Association of Lighting Designer's ETC Award. Recent designs include *Anansi the Spider; Aesop's Fables* (Unicorn Theatre); *World's End* (King's Head Theatre); *I'll Take You To Mrs. Cole* (Complicite); *Whitewash* (Soho Theatre); *The Actor's Nightmare* (Park Theatre); *Mapping Brent* (Kiln Theatre); *Mary's Babies* (Jermyn Street Theatre); *Glory* (Duke's Theatre/Red Ladder); *Cuzco* (Theatre503); *The Hoes* (Hampstead Theatre); *Losing Venice* (Orange Tree Theatre); *King Lear, Lorna Doone* (Exmoor National Park); *A Lie of the Mind* (Southwark Playhouse); *46 Beacon* (Trafalgar Studios with Rick Fisher); *Out There on Fried Meat Ridge Road* (White Bear Theatre/Trafalgar Studios 2); *Acorn* (Courtyard Theatre. Off-West End Award nomination for Best Lighting).

Sound Designer – Anna Clock

Anna Clock is a composer, sound designer and cellist working across theatre, film, radio and installation. Recent projects include: *I WANNA BE YOURS* (Paines Plough & Tamasha); *ADMIN* (Vault, Live Collision, Dublin Fringe festivals); *Playing*

Up and *Epic Stages* (National Youth Theatre); *Armadillo* (The Yard Theatre); *Fighter* (Stratford Circus Arts Centre); *Looking Forward* (Battersea Arts Centre); *Soft Animals* (Soho Theatre); *The Butterfly Lion* (Barn Theatre); *Fatty Fat Fat* (Camden Roundhouse, Edinburgh Festival); *WORK BITCH; Miss Fortunate* (VAULT Festival); *Twelfth Night* (Southwark Playhouse); *Pomona; Punk Rock* (New Diorama); *Bury The Dead* (Finborough Theatre); *Fabric* (Soho Theatre & Community spaces tour); *Katie Johnstone; In The Night Time; [BLANK]* (Orange Tree Theatre); *Overexposed* (V & A Museum); *UN-CENSORED* (Royal Haymarket Theatre); *Songlines* (Edinburgh & HighTide Festivals, Regional Tour); *Finding Fassbender* (Vault, Edinburgh & HighTide Festivals). In 2018, Anna was artist in residence at SPINE Festival Borough of Harrow and Sirius Arts Centre.

Anna studied Music Composition and English Literature at Trinity College Dublin, Cello performance at the Royal Irish Academy of Music and holds an MA in Advanced Theatre Practice from Central School of Speech and Drama.
www.annaclock.com

Movement Director – Diane Alison-Mitchell

Diane is a movement director/theatre choreographer. Recent theatre credits include: *Wife, Holy Sh!t* (Kiln Theatre); *Our Lady of Kibeho* (Royal & Derngate); *The Hoes* (Hampstead Theatre); *Never Vera Blue, Offside* (Futures Theatre); *The Island* (Theatre Chipping Norton/Dukes Lancaster); *Roundelay, Klippies* (Southwark Playhouse); *They Drink It In The Congo* (Almeida Theatre); *SOUL* (Royal & Derngate/Hackney Empire); *Othello, Julilus Caesar* (RSC); *How Nigeria Became* (Unicorn Theatre); *The Gershwin's Porgy and Bess* (Regent's Park Open Air Theatre); *We Are Proud to Present* (Bush Theatre); *The Island* (Young Vic). As a director, Diane co-directed *Bones* by Tanika Gupta at the Courtyard Theatre, Royal Central.

Casting Director – Nadine Rennie CDG

Nadine was in-house Casting Director at Soho Theatre for fifteen years; working on new plays by writers including Dennis Kelly, Bryony Lavery, Arinze Kene, Philip Ridley, Laura Wade and Vicky Jones. Directors she has worked with include Tamara Harvey, Indu Rubasingham, Michael Buffong and Roxanna Silbert. Since going freelance in January 2019, Nadine has worked for Arcola Theatre (*Hoard* & *The Glass Menagerie*); Leeds Playhouse (*There Are No Beginnings*); Sheffield Crucible (*The Last King of Scotland*); Orange Tree Theatre (*Little Baby Jesus*); and continues to cast for Soho Theatre. TV work includes BAFTA winning CBBC series DIXI (casting first three series).

Nadine also has a long running association as Casting Director for Synergy Theatre Project and is a member of the Casting Directors Guild.

Grace Lewis – Company Stage Manager

Grace trained at University of Reading and Mountview Academy of Theatre Arts. Theatre credits include: *The Sweet Science of Bruising* (Wilton's Music Hall & Southwark Playhouse); *WarHorse* (International 2019 – 2020 Tour); *Billy Bishop Goes to War* (Southwark Playhouse); *Men & Girls Dance* (The Place); *Trojan Horse* (Blue Elephant); *3Women, Rasheeda Speaking and The Red Lion* (Trafalgar Studios); *After the Ball* (Upstairs at the Gatehouse); *By the Bog of Cats and Tess of the D'Urbervilles* (Bernie Grant Arts Centre); The Living River (BAC); *Food and Plague Over England* (Finborough Theatre); *We Raise Our Hands in the Sanctuary* (The Albany); *The Stronger and Storm* (Jermyn Street Theatre); *The Cardinal* (Southwark Playhouse); *Counting Stars* (Theatre Royal Stratford East); *Welcome to Thebes* (Bridewell Theatre); Jane Eyre (Jacksons Lane); *Three More Sleepless Nights, Carve* (Tristan Bates Theatre); *I am a Superhero, White People* (Theatre503); and *Divine Humanity* (Charing Cross Theatre). Grace is also Head of Stage Management at National Youth Theatre.

SOHO THEATRE

Soho Theatre is London's most vibrant venue for new theatre, comedy and cabaret with a national and international touring programme, a digital presence and an additional venue in progress. As entrepreneurial as we are innovative, under the leadership of Executive Director Mark Godfrey and Creative Director David Luff, our charity and social enterprise's mission is to produce new work, discover and nurture new writers and artists, and target and develop new audiences.

We work with artists in a variety of ways, from full producing of new plays, to co-producing new work, working with associate artists and presenting the best new emerging theatre companies that we can find.

We have numerous artists on attachment and under commission, including Soho Six and a thriving Company of writers and comedy groups. We read and see hundreds of scripts and shows a year.

'The place was buzzing, and there were queues all over the building as audiences waited to go into one or other of the venue's spaces... exuberant and clearly anticipating a good time.' Guardian.

We attract over 240,000 audience members a year at Soho Theatre, at festivals and through our national and international touring. We produced, co-produced or staged over 40 new plays in the last 12 months.

As an entrepreneurial charity and social enterprise, we have created an innovative and sustainable business model. We maximise value from Arts Council England and philanthropic funding, contributing more to government in tax and NI than we receive in public funding.

Registered Charity No: 267234

Soho Theatre, 21 Dean Street
London W1D 3NE
Admin 020 7287 5060
Box Office 020 7478 0100

LOTTERY FUNDED | Supported using public funding by
ARTS COUNCIL ENGLAND

OPPORTUNITIES FOR WRITERS AT SOHO THEATRE

We are looking for unique and unheard voices – from all backgrounds, attitudes and places.

We want to make things you've never seen before.

Alongside workshops, readings and notes sessions, there are several ways writers can connect with Soho Theatre. You can

Enter our prestigious biennial competition the **Verity Bargate Award** just as **Vicky Jones** did in 2013 with her Award-winning first play *The One*.

Participate in our nine month long Writers' Labs programme, where we will take you through a three-draft process.

Submit your script to submissions@sohotheatre.com where your play will go directly to our Artistic team

Invite us to see your show via coverage@sohotheatre.com

We consider every submission for production or any of the further development opportunities.

sohotheatre.com

Keep up to date:

sohotheatre.com
@sohotheatre all social media

Cassiopeia Berkeley-Agyepong
Simone Ibbett-Brown

SHUCK 'N' JIVE

OBERON BOOKS
LONDON

WWW.OBERONBOOKS.COM

First published in 2019 by Oberon Books Ltd
521 Caledonian Road, London N7 9RH
Tel: +44 (0) 20 7607 3637 / Fax: +44 (0) 20 7607 3629
e-mail: info@oberonbooks.com
www.oberonbooks.com

PB ISBN: 9781786829429
E ISBN: 9781786829412

Cover design by Conor Jatter

Her name is a sweet thing
A name she never owned
Pretending
To tell a story

A rehearsed reading of the play, under the working title *The Next Jessye Norman*, featured in the Blacktress Season at the Tristan Bates Theatre in December 2018 with the following cast:

SIMONE	Esme Laudat
CASSI	Merryl Ansah
BENNY	Martha Pothen

Shuck 'n' Jive was workshopped at the Soho Theatre in April 2019 with the following cast:

SIMONE	Esme Laudat
CASSI	Aretha Ayeh
BENNY	Martha Pothen

Characters

(In order of appearance)

SIMONE

25, Vegan, Mezzo-Soprano, Mixed-Race
(East Anglian and Jamaican), Mid-Essex accent
(or any other non-RP, non-London, UK accent)

CASSI

24, Londoner, Mezzo-Soprano, Black (Ghanaian and
Grenadian), Standard English accent (Lazy RP
with hints of Multicultural London English)

The characters detailed below can be played by
additional actors or multi-roled by the actors playing
SIMONE and CASSI:

PANELIST
CASTING DIRECTOR
CASTING ASSISTANT
MUSICAL DIRECTOR
VOICEOVER
JOHNNY
MALE ENSEMBLE
GAME SHOW HOST
BITTER ACTRESS 1/2
NEWSREADER
TUBE LADY VOICE
DSM
AUDIENCE MEMBER 1/2/3/4
PRODUCER
PERSON
RECEPTIONIST

PERFORMANCE NOTES

A / indicates an interruption

Unbracketed italicised text indicates sung lyrics or spoken word

Italicised bold text should be spoken simultaneously

All scenes should be accompanied by music or a soundscape, except 2.2 which should be played in silence

The music chosen to accompany 1.0 and 1.19 should be the same

The music chosen to accompany 1.7, 1.8 and 1.10 should be the same

The music chosen to accompany 1.11 and 1.13 should be the same

The music chosen to accompany 2.8 should be the same as, or in some way mirror, the music used in 1.1

This text went to press before the end of rehearsals and so may differ slightly from the play as performed

Part One

ZERO

Music is playing.

The audience enter.

ONE

SIMONE: Hello.

CASSI: Heya.

SIMONE: Hi.

    ...

    I'm Simone, I'm a vegan, I was born and raised in East Anglia.

CASSI: I'm Cassi, I grew up in South London watching Lizzie the puppet on *Playdays* and it's easier to say I'm from South London, but I'm actually from Croydon and the side of Croydon that's basically Surrey so not London at all really I guess...

BOTH: We are best friends.

They begin to dance or enact some choreographed movement in time and in keeping stylistically with the music. Like arm-only yoga, or Solange's bandmates. The movements are universal but the routine is unique to them.

    We love music.

    ...

    And we love the theatre:

CASSI: its power to move

SIMONE: and to teach

CASSI: to change a mind,

SIMONE: open a heart,

CASSI: eye,

SIMONE: mouth,

CASSI: pocket,

SIMONE: to communicate

CASSI: live*

SIMONE: something to a group of people who may never have met each other,

CASSI: sat next to each other,

SIMONE: treat** each other like human beings with minds and feelings just like them –

CASSI: another qualia-soaked, newly behoped –

SIMONE: by something dope

CASSI: like theatre

SIMONE: or music;

CASSI: if it hadn't been for theatre

SIMONE: or iPlayer

CASSI: or Netflix

SIMONE: or music

---

* *adverb – pronunciation should rhyme with 'jive'*
** *past tense – pronunciation should rhyme with 'met'*

BOTH: or something that doesn't know what it is

   …

   like this.

   …

   We spend our lives jiving

CASSI: metaphorically

SIMONE: 'cause this is actually quite tiring.

CASSI: We travel up and down the city,

SIMONE: county,

CASSI: sovereign state

SIMONE: and nation

CASSI: singing, dancing, acting,

SIMONE: hoping to put something either fun or good into the world

CASSI: the only way we know how

SIMONE: the best way we know how.

CASSI: We always have a story

SIMONE: so if you don't lose patience with our fumbling around

CASSI: we'll come up singing for you, even when we're down.

SIMONE: Oh, and we text each other a lot.

They stop dancing, or dance more, and a phone pings with every text that comes through.

SIMONE: About work:

CASSI: Just got an audition through for the role of 'God' – not sure it's my casting but the script is funny.

About where we are:

SIMONE: Waiting for an Uber with thirty kilograms of pebbles, a wheelie bed and a packet of chips.

About people:

CASSI: My dad and brother just spent the last half hour discussing which of them would have got gunged on *Get Your Own Back*.

SIMONE: Well, the first thing we need to know is who has the greater command of late '90s general knowle–

CASSI: About music and theatre and nothing at all:

SIMONE: OMG can you send me a tune – I've had this bit in my head from *Makropulos Case* – it's this supernatural backstage musical murder mystery thriller – actually don't, I love it.

CASSI: Yas.

OMG Fairfield Halls has reopened!

SIMONE:

CASSI: It's the theatre in Croydon. We should go.

SIMONE: YASSSSSS.

OMG my autocorrect autocorrects 'yes' to YASSSSS.

CASSI: …

BOTH: YASSSSSSSSSSSS.

…

They do the laugh-sigh.

SIMONE: So I walk in and Paul, the accompanist, is wearing a print of Hieronymus Bosch's *Garden of Earthly Delights* – it gives the impression at first glance that it's a back, front and full sleeves full-colour tatt, and that he's naked from the waist up, with tortured faces on his nipples –

THREE

The music stops. The lighting shifts – we are in her audition room.

PANELIST: Hello? I said what role would you like to sing in six months' time?

SIMONE: Uh, sorry! Well, chorus in *Porgy and Bess,* I suppose.

PANELIST: Right. What have you brought for us?

SIMONE: I've got some Czech? Or a French aria –

PANELIST: Okay. Let's hear that then.

SIMONE: Thank you.

SIMONE begins to sing Offenbach's 'The Doll Song', which morphs into F. Dumont & J. Stewart's 'I Want to See The Old Home', at which point there is a transformation into the magical world of the stage. By the end of the number we have reached a single spotlight, glitter, quick change (featuring minstrel gloves) territory…

Les oiseaux dans la charmille
Dans les cieux l'astre du jour
Tout parle à la jeune fille
Tout parle à la jeune fille d'amour
Tout parle d'amour

Voilà la chanson gentille
La chanson d'Olympia, d'Olympia
Ah!

I've wandered very far away
From the clime where I was born
And my poor heart has been so sad,
Dejected and forlorn;
No master kind to treat me well,
To cheer me when in pain,
I want to see the cotton fields,
And the dear old home again

When I was free, I left that land,
Where the days are bright and fair,
Where Massa spoke to me so kind,
When I was bow'd with care;
I left that home no friends to find,
My heart was fill'd with pain
Oh! take me to that good old home,
To see it once again

Oh, the good old days are pass'd and gone,

I sigh for them in vain;
I want to see the cotton fields,
And the dear old home again

PANELIST: –

SIMONE: –

PANELIST: Never bring this song to an audition again

SIMONE: –

PANELIST: because you are not a soprano.

FOUR

Traffic sounds.

CASSI: To be fair it doesn't sound like they didn't like you.

SIMONE: Yeah apart from when I just stared at Paul's T-shirt for ten minutes it actually went really well and they were all super lovely so, even if nothing comes of it, I don't think I did anything too weird.

CASSI: Mate I'm sure you were fine. I'm here by the way, table in the corner.

Traffic sounds fade into ambient cafe sounds.

SIMONE: How's the show?

CASSI: Lol. Can we not. It's like I become semi-human again when I'm not stuck on tour, allow me these two days of sanity.

SIMONE: *(Looking at phone.)* Sorry I just need to sort this. Have you got any ideas of where to put on a semi-staged performance of *The Makropulos Case*?

CASSI: For cheap? I saw a post about a scratch night in a couple of weeks –

SIMONE: It's got a cast of forty.

CASSI: – or you could try the National Theatre?

SIMONE: Ah but Janáček didn't release a moderately successful pop album in the late '90s so –

CASSI: Savageeee.

iPhone ping, Apple Watch vibration, pop-up sound on MacBook.

SIMONE: Wow, Cassi, I think you might have a message there?

CASSI: You've watched *She's Gotta Have It*, right?

SIMONE: Obviously.

CASSI: So I might have matched with a girl on Hinge who looks like exactly like DeWanda Wise.

SIMONE: Sorry what.

CASSI: I know I am freaking out. And like ignoring the fact she is stunning, just look at her messages. She has somehow mastered that intangible balance of casual intellectualism, feminist wiles and flirtatious banter. I am ready to marry.

SIMONE: So, are you going to meet her?

CASSI: Absolutely not.

SIMONE: What?! Why?

CASSI: Never meet your heroes, Simone.

SIMONE: Oh. My. God. Message her now.

CASSI: What if I'm being catfished?

SIMONE: Well, if your catfisher /

CASSI: Aren't they just a catfish?

SIMONE: – has mastered that intangible balance of casual intellectualism, feminist wiles and flirtatious banter, maybe your catfish is worth meeting anyway? I'm kidding – do you think you might be being catfished? Report her. REPORT.

CASSI: I never report any of my online stalkers.

SIMONE: A. That's terrible on many levels but we'll discuss that later. B. Stop deflecting.

CASSI: She's just too perfect. Like I know my attraction to women is rooted in narcissism but also I can't actually go out with someone more attractive than me.

SIMONE: I bet she's simply a complementary level of attractive. Like orange and purple.

CASSI: Orange and purple do go really well together.

iPhone ping, Apple Watch vibration, pop-up sound on MacBook.

SIMONE: OMG is that her? What did she say?

CASSI: Oh my god, / oh my god, oh my god.

SIMONE: What does it say?

CASSI: No, no, it's an audition…for *Hamlet (The Musical).*

SIMONE: *Hamlet.* The Musical.

CASSI: 1. The implicit disdain in your tone was noted and is not appreciated 2. I have legit been OBSESSED with Ophelia since I was about thirteen years old. We had to bring a poem to audition for our school production of *The Sound of Music* in year nine and whilst everyone else was doing their best recitation of 'On the Ning Nang Nong' I of course rocked up and did a fully staged extract of Ophelia's mad songs –

SIMONE: Brilliant.

CASSI: – giving it the full:

'Tomorrow is Saint Valentine's Day…
They say the owl was a baker's daughter…
Goodnight ladies
Goodnight sweet ladies
Goodnight
Goodnight.'

And I mean I won't go into the multitude of tenuous links I can retroactively draw between Maria and Ophelia to try and justify my choice of 'poem'.

SIMONE: Please tell me your teachers saw the 'get thee to a nunnery...' parallels.

CASSI: Yeah but they somehow missed my leading lady potential. I was cast as one of one hundred fifty ensemble nuns.

SIMONE takes CASSI's phone and begins to scan through her email.

SIMONE: 'We're looking for a diverse cast to bring a new musical re-imagining of *Hamlet* to UK audiences.'

CASSI: Fab. Excellent. Good, yes.

SIMONE: 'We are particularly keen to cast actors from a BAME background for this project.'

CASSI: 'Black, Asian and Minority Ethnic' is not a singular 'background' but we can dismantle this after you've cast me as Ophelia.

SIMONE: Yaaassss. 'The music in the piece will be gospel slash Motown slash soul. Please prepare two contrasting songs from these genres.'

CASSI: Okay wait. So the new musically re-imagined version of Ophelia can only be black if she sounds like the second-coming of Whitney?

SIMONE: Ay, there's the rub.

CASSI: They always do this. Literally my rep folder is a love letter to Harold Arlen and all they want to hear is 'I believe the children are our future'. And yes that is a classic tune. But also I can sing other things Simone. / Let me sing other things please just this one time –

SIMONE: Mate I didn't write this casting breakdown. Also gospel slash Motown slash soul *Hamlet* is v different to like I dunno –

CASSI: – *give me one moment in time where I don't have to sound like Whitney when all / of my dreams –*

SIMONE: You need to calm down.

CASSI: Gah. Fine. It's Ophelia. Can ya press reply and type this to my agent: 'This looks really exciting exclamation mark exclamation mark exclamation mark. Just confirming that I can make it to the audition at twelve p.m. next Monday full stop.'

FIVE

The music stops. The lighting shifts – we are in her audition room.

CASTING DIRECTOR: Hello Cassi, lovely to see you again.

CASSI: It's Naomi. She's a big Casting Director. One of the ones they got in to hear us sing at drama school. Seven months ago I kind of got the impression that she liked me? But she's so hard to read that who really knows.

Hiya! How're you?

'How're you.' Like we're bezzie mates. Gah why am I like this?!

CASTING DIRECTOR: Great. Thanks.

CASTING ASSISTANT: I love your full name by the way. Cassiopeia? Is that how you say it? So nice.

CASSI: The casting assistant, all smiles and a ponytail and a face that actually says: 'We were casting this all last week as well and if I have to listen to another person singing 'I Wanna Dance With Somebody' I might cry.'

Ah thank you so / much.

CASTING DIRECTOR: I think you've met Rachel, my assistant, and this is Matt, our MD.

MUSICAL DIRECTOR: Hi.

CASTING DIRECTOR: What have you brought to sing for us?

CASSI: 'Run to You' by Whitney Houston or 'Unpretty' by TLC.

Always lead with the song you actually want to sing and slightly speed up and lower your volume when you say the title of the second one so that they just go with the first.

MUSICAL DIRECTOR: Cool, we'll have the Whitney. What kind of tempo do you want for this?

CASSI: Matt the MD has the most gorgeous hazel eyes. In times gone by, many a beautiful man has distracted me from my dreams, but this time 'round I made sure to Google the creative team in advance. Winning.

Oh it's like, *I know that when you look at me...*

MUSICAL DIRECTOR: Awesome. Whenever you're ready.

CASSI begins to sing J. Friedman and A. Rich's 'Run to You'. As before, the song morphs into a minstrel tune, S. Foster's 'Massa's In De Cold Ground', at which point there is a transformation into the magical world of the stage. By the end of the number we have reached a single spotlight, glitter, quick-change (featuring minstrel gloves) territory...

CASSI:

I know that when you look at me
There's so much that you just don't see
But if you would only take the time
I know in my heart you'd find

Okay so Naomi is nodding her head along to the beat, and Rachel is sending a text message. Maybe they haven't noticed how painfully mediocre this is.

I feel so all alone
I wanna run to you (oooh)
I wanna run to you (oooh)
Won't you hold me in your arms
And keep me safe from harm

Safe to say this is not my finest work. Why do I always shit all over the auditions for the jobs I actually want? Okay still time to save this.

I wanna r–

Round de meadows am a ringing,
De darkey's mournful song,
While de mocking bird am singing,
Happy as de day am long.
Where de ivy am a creeping,
O'er de grassy mound,
Dare old massa am a sleeping,
Sleeping in de cold, cold ground.

Massa make de darkeys love him,
Cayse he was so kind,
Now, dey sadly weep above him,
Mourning cayse he leave dem behind.
I cannot work before tomorrow,
Cayse de teardrop flow
I try to drive away my sorrow,
Pickir on de old banjo

Down in de cornfield
Hear dat mournful sound:
All de darkeys am a weeping,
Massa's in de cold, cold ground

CASTING DIRECTOR: Oh wow, how empowering. Great. Thanks. Well it was lovely to see you again Cassi.

CASTING ASSISTANT: It's actually pronounced 'Cassiopeia'.

CASTING DIRECTOR: Oh.

CASSI: Actually the vowel stress depends on where you... Never mind.

SIX

CASSI: 86 from Chorlton to Manchester Palace.

SIMONE: Eighth circle of hell, i.e. Central line, on my way to Stroud Green.

CASSI: So it's been five days and I am 'disappointed but not surprised' that I haven't heard back from *Hamlet (The Musical)*.

SIMONE: Did you actually want to do it? I mean the street dance battle between Rosencrantz and Guildenstern makes literally no sense.

CASSI: Let's be real, it was all misguided. But I dunno... It would have been nice to be in a show with people who weren't wildly prejudiced.

SIMONE: Ah, shit, I'm sorry.

CASSI: Like I mentioned in passing that I had to take some time out from my degree and next thing I know there's a rumour going 'round the cast that I was kicked out of drama school for dealing drugs on campus.

SIMONE: I thought we'd be free from stuff like this in London.

CASSI: I'm not in London right now. But someone once told me we'd be free from stuff like this in the theatre.

20

Obviously they were wrong. You know I feel like after this job it might be time to just leave it –

SIMONE: It just depends on who's making the theatre. There must be something out there with decent people that isn't an 'urban' retelling of a story about a posh family from four hundred years ago.

CASSI: Well, when you find it give me a call.

SIMONE: Who says you have to find it? When you could make it!

CASSI: And that's a feasible solution, how?

SIMONE: A. Theatre about things that are relevant to real people. B. Theatre about important things and, best of all, C. No accusations of drug dealing or white colleagues who think saying the N-word is okay.

CASSI: Wait who thinks the N-word is okay?

SIMONE: We'll come back to that later – in the play you're going to write!

CASSI: I mean it's not a terrible idea. It could be like us. On stage. And all the conversations we have about the hilarious ridiculous shit that happens that the world just doesn't understand as being absolutely wild.

SIMONE: So you're going to write it then.

CASSI: Incorrect. *We* are going to write it. So. Excited.

SIMONE: Oh, I don't really have much time for stuff at the moment unless it's, like, paid.

CASSI: We could invite producers and sell tickets and get some money from it that way. It needs to be seen by people.

SIMONE: I suppose it would be really nice for us to do it together…

CASSI: Yassss! There's that scratch night happening next month – that would be perfect.

SIMONE: Oh does that pay?

CASSI: Can't we spend the next few weeks working on it, just up until that scratch night and then see what happens?

SIMONE: Do you think we could do a whole play by then?

CASSI: I mean if it's just our lives then it'll basically write itself, right?

SIMONE: Mind you, we're literally never in the same place at the same time, you should / just –

CASSI: So fine. I'll make a shared file on Google Docs.

SIMONE: Ah, the magic of technology, gr9. Sorry typo. Gr8. xoxo

SEVEN

VOICEOVER: One week later.

SIMONE: Delayed train to Winchester.

CASSI: Which one of your million jobs are you travelling to today?

SIMONE: Oh my god so, why I'm no longer talking to white people about anything, not just race.

Phone ping.

JOHNNY: Simone hun, Toggs just mentioned you were in *Hamilton.* CONGRATSSSSSS. So do you get tickets or what.

SIMONE: *Hamilton?* And who is Toggs?

After a bit of research I discovered that Toggs is in fact just Tom McGovern from my opera course.

CASSI: ...*Hamilton*? The new opera *Hamilton* with opera singers in it?

SIMONE: I'm getting to that. So I asked Tom about this –

CASSI: I am deceased.

SIMONE: – and apparently *another* white public schoolboy from my course –

CASSI: Crying with laughter emoji.

SIMONE: – told him – that I was in *Hamilton.*

CASSI: WTF. How? Why? So many questions.

SIMONE: I feel like somebody got confused with *Porgy and Bess*?

CASSI: OF COURSE.

SIMONE: 'She's in the / black people one.'

CASSI: 'She's in the black people one.' Yes.

SIMONE: Even more tragically, I feel like the person who got confused IS SOMEONE I DATED FOR A FUCKING MONTH.

CASSI: And he thought you were in *Hamilton.* The whole time.

SIMONE: We talked about what I thought of it when I went to see it. I mean I'm flattered.

CASSI: I love that. Just doing a show watch. Before the cast change you know.

SIMONE: Yeah, exacte, gotta learn my tracks, come prepared. We're no longer dating by the way... Not 'cause of this.

EIGHT.

VOICEOVER: Two weeks later.

CASSI: Outside Wetherspoons in Sunderland.

SIMONE: Yay did you actually go out for drinks with cast?

CASSI: Oh my god Simone. I can't even. So four of my delightful, cisgender, heterosexual, white, male colleagues just decided to sit me down in the pub and explain that the diversity problem in theatre is solved because – and I quote –

MALE ENSEMBLE: Black people have *Hamilton* and *The Lion King*.

SIMONE: OMG.

CASSI: I was just sat there like do I call this out and burn all my bridges now or just say nothing? Like imagine my shock when they just launched into their spontaneous TED Talk on Post-Racial Performance Art. Forget about in-yer-face theatre. We've moved on to in-yer-face racism.

SIMONE: That surprisingly large intersection of people whose interests include Berkoff and Nigel Farage…

CASSI: And do you know what's even more funny? They thought I was going to agree with them! That I'd sit there and go, 'Yes you are so right! Why are the blacks complaining after years of type-casting and tokenism? Isn't it Political-Correctness-gone-mad for us to expect creative teams to consider casting people who aren't white in stories which aren't specifically about race when your sister wasn't allowed to wear fake tan to play Anita in the local production of *West Side Story*?! God. The injustice!'

NINE

Aggressively cheery Game Show Theme Tune is blaring.

GAME SHOW HOST: Hello and welcome to *Fine 'Cause We're Friends* – the social interaction quiz that simply everyone is talking about. Today we have Simone from Suffolk.

SIMONE: Hi!

GAME SHOW HOST: And Cassi from Croydon.

CASSI: Hiya!

GAME SHOW HOST: The rules are simple: we give our contestants scenarios and they let us know whether it's 'not okay' or 'fine 'cause we're friends'. Remember, don't be too sensitive – after all it's the most agreeable negro who wins the day!

So here we go with our first situation: 'You've got a swanky new up-do and are loving life. Your friend exclaims "Oh my god I love your hair – can I touch it?" but their hands are already all up in your afro.'

CASSI: Sorry did I miss the part where this friend was also my hairdresser?

SIMONE: *(Presses klaxon.)* Fine 'cause we're friends IF I've previously established that I actively like them touching my hair.

GAME SHOW HOST: That's the spirit Simone! You lead with ten points. It's time for scenario two: 'You're hosting a fancy dress party. Your friend has come as Beyoncé's 'Crazy In Love', in cut-off denim short shorts, a white tank top, and yes you guessed it, brown foundation all over their arms, legs and face.'

SIMONE: –

CASSI: –

GAME SHOW HOST: Oh come on now, it's just a bit of fun! Well folks, no points for anyone there. Three: 'You're on a road trip, and your friend is rapping along with the radio and starts shouting the N-word. You ask them to stop, 'cause you're being a bit of an ol' buzzkill there, and they say, "Why do you have to ruin everything, you / black bitch –"'

SIMONE: Er, can we change the channel?

TEN

VOICEOVER: Three weeks later.

CASSI: – because 'Black' is a hyper-adjective which actually tells you an invaluable amount about a person's personality, upbringing, political views, favourite Netflix series, and how spicy they have their chicken in Nando's. And that's all you need to assume to insult them on first meeting right?

But then they'll turn around and be like 'mate y u so obsessed with race tho'.

SIMONE: *(Laughs.)* And then when I say something like 'I did a Stomzy song at church yesterday' I realise that the people I go to school with actually heard 'I was black at church yesterday'.

CASSI laughs.

And then I have to remind them again that I am a vegan so NO I DO NOT EAT CHICKEN.

CASSI: *(Still laughing.)* I was black at church.

SIMONE: 'I tried that vegan chicken restaurant yesterday it was sick' equals 'I tried that vegan *I am black* restaurant yesterday it was *black*.' To be fair I was black at church… mixed race, eh.

CASSI: Do you think we'd be successful if I just wrote 'we am black' a hundred times for every answer in this funding application?

SIMONE: Yeah, that might translate back to 'we are poor' in their heads, sorry, I mean 'we are po'.

CASSI: Well that's sorted then. Also vegan chicken? Do they just season plants as if they were chicken?

SIMONE: Yeah it's stuff called seitan – it's amazing! And they do hot wings, popcorn chicken, chicken burgers, everything.

CASSI: Yasss magical vegan chicken place. Let's go.

SIMONE: And then not tell anyone. Or tell everyone. I don't know how to relate to my black persona anymore.

CASSI: Don't worry just put on Apple Music's Essential Neo-Soul playlist because hello, your name is Simone, and you am black.

ELEVEN

SIMONE: I just don't know if that last segment is a bit glib (I love the word glib) considering, you know, words are important. Expression of identity is important.

CASSI: Hashtag live your truth.

SIMONE: Lol.

CASSI: I know by the end we were being super blasé but I really liked dem words that we dun just wrote.

SIMONE: Well, yeah, I think, I do too, but is it a play if we just string together a load of random conversations we had because we like the way they sound?

CASSI: No...

SIMONE: What's our aim? For the play. In the play. Why are we doing this?

CASSI: Because our lives are hilarious.

SIMONE: Of course. But if they're just structureless conversations it'll just...feel...

CASSI: Structureless.

SIMONE: Yes.

CASSI: Like this... Conversation.

SIMONE: Yes. It needs to be going somewhere.

CASSI: Well, shall we put in a conversation about structuring the play?

SIMONE: Why? How would that get us anywhere?

CASSI: Where are we even trying to go?

SIMONE: To. A place...where...

CASSI: *'There's a place for us'*

SIMONE: YES. Exactly. The play should take us and the audience to a place where there's a place for us and everyone. And nobody has to be in *The Lion King* if they don't want. Or can't.

CASSI: What, like a post-racial society? Simples.

SIMONE: So. Is the play just a series of anecdotes about race?

CASSI: Yeah full of those 'gotta laugh or else I'll cry' moments that typify our existence.

SIMONE: That'd be like pulling teeth.

BOTH: Oh.

SIMONE: I think the main problem for me is that I hate plays that are about what they're actually about.

CASSI: Dunno if you noticed but we've just spent a hella long time writing a play which is two black women talking about being black women.

SIMONE: I know...

CASSI: And you didn't think to say something after the first scene, or the fifth...

SIMONE: ...

CASSI: Wow. *(Beat.)* You know I feel like this is probably the closest we've ever come to disagreeing on something. But I've actually been thinking for a few days that what this whole thing is lacking is conflict. Like you can't have seventy-six minutes of us just agreeing with each other.

SIMONE: YES. But I don't know if that comes from a disagreement between us necessarily though – it could be a disagreement between us and our past selves or our future selves or...

Like I don't think an argument scene is our vibe unless it's about something actually non-race related. I just can't imagine what would be high stakes enough.

CASSI: ...

Do you have a strong opinion on irregular rhyme?

SIMONE: God, we're such one-dimensional characters. All we talk about is theatre. And race. We are literally walking talking stereotypes. But, you know, intersectional ones – hipsters *and* black people. Blipsters.

CASSI: So currently we're creating something akin to a three-minute song Bernstein wrote sixty years ago, which has no semblance of a plot, but *is* enacted by two black women who only talk angrily about race.

SIMONE: Someone get me a ticket now. We need the conflict to be something non-surface level – a difference in who we are as people.

CASSI: Hashtag we are not a monolith.

SIMONE: You use more hashtags in real life than you do on the internet. *Lungs.* Two people try to do something together but something's in the middle.

CASSI: Your trachea.

SIMONE: They try to ignore it but that trachea eventually sparks an argument, an argument not of opinion, but years of miscommunication and false belief about the nature of the friendship, and the crushing moment of realisation that it's a sham you've constructed for yourselves separately and together. People-not-understanding-each-other-to-their-very-core type things.

CASSI: Like I said – do you have a strong opinion on irregular rhyme?

SIMONE: Like… We don't finish the play.

They take that in. Does it stop right n–

Or we do but it's years later or only one of us finished it 'cause we hate each other.

CASSI: *Merrily We Roll Along*-style.

30

SIMONE: OR ONE OF US DIED. 'Cause they didn't have papers.

CASSI: No one needs to die.

SIMONE: Because of Windrush. We're turned away by the NHS and we're secretly seventy.

CASSI: You know, having seen *Fun Home,* the anti-happy ending is my new obsession.

SIMONE: Don't tell me the ending to *Fun Home.* Please, Cassi, no spoilers. OMG this is our big argument, right here.

They are suddenly arguing.

CASSI: BABE, THEY TELL YOU THE END AT THE START. BUT THAT'S ALL I'M GOING TO SAY.

SIMONE: THANK YOU, I REALLY APPRECIATE THAT.

Back to normal.

CASSI: Yeah, I think that would be a good mini argument to have. We need some of those peppered in before the explosion.

Phone pings.

SIMONE: My friend's just had a really good idea for the title of the show: *Dear White Producers.*

VOICEOVER: For those not in the know, this refers to the Netflix series *Dear White People,* itself referring to the eponymous radio show within the TV show –

CASSI: *(Waves at VOICEOVER to be quiet.)* Oh my god or just a section of the show. Had this idea to do little random breakout moments –

SIMONE: Hashtag generation *Scrubs* and *Family Guy.*

VOICEOVER: Look who's hashtagging now.

SIMONE: You're not in this scene, mate.

CASSI: – like *Microaggression of the Week*, and *Dear White Producers* would be parfait. So we'll end a scene and then it can suddenly be like a face-off style game show.

SIMONE: Or not even fully end the scene…

CASSI: I love that we're taking all our favourite TV moments and putting them on stage –

SIMONE: I guess not…

CASSI: – why don't more people do random cutaways? Like, they are the essence of all digressive storytelling. People are just so focused on a solid narrative through-line that they miss all the fun you can have dancing 'round the path.

SIMONE: Cue cutaway of us explaining that and then a meta cutaway of us dancing 'round a path…

CASSI: Even the random trip to Cuba in *Guys and Dolls* is qualified by the plot –

SIMONE: I guess not…

CASSI: How much better would it be if they were just suddenly in Cuba purely for the LOLs?

SIMONE: It would be so meta… Cutawayception!

Begin segue into cutaway.

Not that that's what that suffix means…

Oh my god. I think it's happening!

TWELVE

The intro to 'Lizzie's Song' begins. Strings are attached to CASSI's hands, elbows, knees, feet and head as she becomes Lizzie, the singing/ dancing puppet from her childhood. What follows is a bizarrely accurate performance of the puppet's dance routine from the Children's BBC series Playdays. *SIMONE ad-libs responses.*

THIRTEEN

As if nothing has happened.

CASSI: So meta. Hilarious. Yes. That's definitely got to go in.

SIMONE: You do realise that your premier black woman role model was literally a puppet controlled by a white man, right?

CASSI: I did not come here to be judged. We've got two weeks until that scratch night. We'll fully have this play finished by then, won't we?

SIMONE: Yeah. Maybe. Yeah, I reckon we can do it – we've got a roll on now!

CASSI: *'Rollin'*

SIMONE: *Rollin'!*

BOTH: *Rollin' on the river!'*

Music kicks in, lights start to change –

SIMONE: No, stop, stop it – we don't have time for this now. We've got a show to do!

CASSI: Wait so I get that the hilarity of everyday racism isn't enough, but what have we even decided? Like what's our aim for the play? Hashtag the big questions.

SIMONE: I'm not sure. Yet. But that's okay – we have two weeks. I'm sure we'll find our muse.

FOURTEEN

Music is muffled by the rumbling and wailing of the Central line.

CASSI: So in addition to being a fiery pit of hell, the Central line is also just like aggressively loud.

BITTER ACTRESS 1: Don't you think there are just sooooo many black shows on at the moment? Like *Motown*, *Tina* / *Lion King*.

BITTER ACTRESS 2: / yeah! And like all the female roles in *Book of Mormon*.

CASSI: I've just met these two girls at a dance call. Apparently we're now best friends.

Throughout the following the Central line gets incrementally louder whenever the actresses say something outrageous. They increase their volume so as to be heard over it.

BITTER ACTRESS 1: And then when shows aren't for black people / they suddenly come out with an 'all-black' version. It's just so unfair. Like I would have loved to play Adelaide in *Guys and Dolls* but wasn't even allowed to audition for that Manchester revival. And it's just such double standards. Like imagine what people would say if I said I wanted to do an 'all-white' version of anything?!

CASSI: / Aren't for black people.

BITTER ACTRESS 2: Oh my god you'd be crucified.

CASSI: Or they'd turn your attention to most of the shows you haven't just mentioned.

BITTER ACTRESS 1: That's right! They'd all say I was 'racist' and it wouldn't be allowed to happen!

CASSI: Actually I think you've got to consider that –

BITTER ACTRESS 1: Also like have they even seen *Hairspray*?! Everyone knows segregation like that ended in the '60s. All it does is make it seem like they can't compete on the same level as people like us. I even have friends where it's like you wouldn't even know they weren't white unless you asked – but they're capitalising on their I dunno 'racial ambiguity' and using it as a free pass into auditions.

CASSI: Is this actually a serious conversation these two women are hav–

BITTER ACTRESS 2: Like think about it, we've been working front of house for what? Two months now…and it's literally just because diversity is the flavour of the month and no one wants to cast us because we're not BAMA or whatever the acronym is. Le sigh.

BITTER ACTRESS 1: Yeah this is exactly what I was trying to say. There are just too many black shows at the minute. Don't you think if we were black we'd be working all the time too?

Central line screaming increases. CASSI screams with it. Flicker-y nightmare lights transform into bright and comforting television studio lights. CASSI's screams abate as a Newsroom Jingle emerges from the ragings of the Central line.

FIFTEEN

NEWSREADER: That was Pete, our political correspondent, and before the weather where you are. It's time for our new segment *Microaggression of the Week*. Human brains are programmed to listen to and respond to stories. Stories make people connect with you. Stories make people appreciate your message. And today we have two women here who have bravely agreed to share their stories and open our eyes to the 'Black Experience'. Now first of all – 'microaggression' what does that 'word' actually 'mean'?

CASSI: So it was a term coined in the 1970s by Dr Chester Pierce, who said that 'racial microaggressions are the brief and everyday slights, insults, indignities and denigrating messages sent to people of colour by well-intentioned white people who are unaware of the hidden messages being communicated.'

SIMONE: Basically these are kind of commonplace things that people might say or do, which are intrinsically linked to racial bias. Now it doesn't matter whether or not they intended to be racist, the nature of a racial microaggression is that their actions or words have communicated a hostile, derogatory or negative racial slight.

NEWSREADER: Okay so that's quite a complex issue for our viewers to understand, maybe you can clear it up with some examples of the things you might encounter on a day-to-day basis:

Circus Theme begins to play.

SIMONE: What are you? No like what's your heritage?

CASSI: Oh my gosh you're quite well-spoken, aren't you?

SIMONE: So glad I have normal hair, I mean it looks awesome on you but I could never look good with all that growing out of my head.

CASSI: Wow I love your dress it's just so exotic.

SIMONE: You know, sometimes I totally forget that you're black.

CASSI: You know, it's the weirdest thing, because you're like really quiet and always reading a book or something, but I still just find you so… intimidating!

SIMONE: So most of the characters are related, but if you were planning to audition I think you'd really be so convincing in the role of the maid.

CASSI: So I've always longed to hear this sung in a less white middle-class kind of way. I think you could really bring something to it.

SIMONE: Don't be silly, they don't have lawnmowers in Africa.

CASSI: That was really great, like really, but this time could you really black it up for me, I need you to just be more sassy, riff the fuck out of it and shout Jesus.

SIMONE: Have you ever considered skin-lightening cream? There are some really great brands.

CASSI: I'm sure you didn't even need to audition for this part –

SIMONE: – or interview for this job –

CASSI: – you just look so right for it, you know?

SIMONE: – the company's really trying to diversify, you know?

Change of channel; the white noise sounds suspiciously like the Central line.

SIXTEEN

Aggressively cheery Game Show Theme Tune is blaring.

GAME SHOW HOST: Hello and welcome back to *Fine 'Cause We're Friends*, the social interaction quiz that simply everyone is nagging the BLEEP out of us about.

SIMONE: Oh god, not this again –

GAME SHOW HOST: Here we go with scenario four: 'You call your friend in floods of tears to tell them that your grandfather has passed away. In response to this tragic news they start to sing 'No Woman, No Cry' down the phone.'

SIMONE:

CASSI:

GAME SHOW HOST: The folks at home are laughing, but our contestants seem to have lost their sense of fun! REMEMBER *don't be too sensitive* – after all it's the most agreeable negro who wins the day!

Five: 'Your friend is training as a beauty therapist and offers to give you a facial. You begin to experience an intense burning sensation all over your face. They very calmly inform you that they've attempted to bleach your skin.'

SIMONE: Stop – stop – wait – this can't go in. *(Accidentally presses the klaxon.)* Shit. I don't think this is – how do you stop this thing?! *(Klaxon stops.)* This isn't good.

CASSI: But wasn't the point to escalate it to a place where obviously none of these things are okay?

SIMONE: Yes, but I – if they're obviously not okay, why are we saying them?

CASSI: Because there'll be some people who actually think they're okay /

SIMONE: Yeah / but –

CASSI: – and others who will appreciate it being said that these things obviously aren't okay.

SIMONE: Yeah. But are we going to teach the people who think it's okay that it's not okay with this? Isn't it a bit intense for an educational device?

CASSI: –

SIMONE: Ignore me. It's a good scene. Sorry, go on.

GAME SHOW HOST: 'They very calmly inform you that they've attempted to bleach your skin.'

SIMONE: Fine 'cause we're friends. *(Presses klaxon.)* Just do the next one…

GAME SHOW HOST: Well done, Simone, that's another point to you!

Scenario SIX! 'You're staying at your friend's house for the weekend. As you head up to bed their mother jovially calls after you to say that she's locked all the jewellery boxes just in case you were thinking of pinching anything to take back and sell on the African black market…'

The host continues talking, their story growing more and more absurd as they are slowly drowned out by a crescendo-ing klaxon.

'…Your friend asks if you know any voodoo rituals that they can use as inspiration for their movement piece. Your friend sends you a photo every single time they come across a box braid on the pavement and asks whether you've lost something. Your friend asks if you know any single black guys they can date to piss off their parents. Your friend says…'

The klaxon merges to become the screaming of the Central line.

SEVENTEEN

Lighting shifts back to Central line.

TUBE LADY VOICE: This is Holborn. Change here for the Piccadilly line.

EIGHTEEN

SIMONE: Oh shit I meant to ask earlier but… Can we take out the name of the opera company?

CASSI: Wait but wasn't the whole idea that they need to be held accountable for their actions.

SIMONE: Well – of course, in general, but not *them* specifically and not right now –

CASSI: Why?

SIMONE: I just feel like if I go out there and say the actual name of the company then I'll never work again.

CASSI: And is that a bad thing if they're heinously racist?

SIMONE: It's not as simple as that though, is it?

CASSI: Come on, it's not like any of them are actually going to see this.

SIMONE: Word gets around, ya know? First you get a name for being troublesome, next thing you're saddled with thousands of pounds of degree debt and no job prospects beyond the local McDonald's, oh no, wait, you're actually overqualified for that job, so that's a no, so yeah, no job prospects.

CASSI: I fully don't understand you sometimes.

SIMONE: I guess anyone who would've known what the company was will still know even if we don't say the name, so let's just leave it as is –

CASSI: If we're just casually re-writing the play at the five, then I have some suggestions too.

SIMONE: We're not, I said let's leave it –

CASSI: In the newsroom scene it's like we're just listing shit that happens. How is that actually doing anything to show people that it's not okay?

SIMONE: I said that last week –

CASSI: And I'm saying it now. So let's change it.

SIMONE: The fact is that our slot is in five minutes and we
    can't keep changing the script.

CASSI: Well you just tried to –

SIMONE: Oh that was barely a change and only to my lines –

DSM: That's clearance. Please stand by.

CASSI: It would have undermined our whole message.

SIMONE: It's either that or I undermine my whole rent.

CASSI: Better to be destitute than a supremacist puppet.

SIMONE: Oh my god what… That's quite a good line.

DSM: Are you ready?

Simultaneously:

CASSI: No.

SIMONE: Yes.

NINETEEN

Music begins to play.

Rapturous applause.

TWENTY

AUDIENCE 1: So refreshing to have two new black voices in
    the theatre.

AUDIENCE 2: It's just so wonderful to see two African-
    American Women on stage.

Circus Theme starts playing in the background.

AUDIENCE 3: You know you reminded me so much of Jessye
    Norman. Such power.

AUDIENCE 4: I just loved the bit where you were speaking about being black.

AUDIENCE 2: But don't you think if you can say the N-word that everyone should be able to say the N-word. Freedom of speech is important.

AUDIENCE 3: Can *I* touch your hair?

AUDIENCE 1: It's so brilliant they let you do your little show here. Diverse programming is the way forward.

AUDIENCE 2: It really was so great. But like what's wrong with being called exotic? That's obviously meant to be a compliment.

AUDIENCE 3: So when are you starting in *Hamilton*?

AUDIENCE 2: I've got a black friend and she loves being called exotic.

PRODUCER: Yeah, loved it – it was great, brilliant. How did you feel it went?

Circus Theme slowly fades out.

CASSI: Well –

PRODUCER: Ahaha, don't say anything, it was obviously just… *(Gestures something good.)*

SIMONE: Oh. Thank you –

PRODUCER: So, I'll cut to the chase. We want to see more. I'll email you tonight but your show, our theatre. Am I wrong? Right. Yes, four-week run, all the trimmings.

CASSI: –

PRODUCER: Great, brilliant. Can't wait to work with you girls. *(Answers phone.)* KP, hit me.

Part Two

ONE

CASSI: Simone. We just got programmed for a four-week run. AHHHHHHH.

SIMONE: I can't even believe the producer came to be honest /

CASSI: NEITHER CAN I.

SIMONE: Based on the treatment

CASSI: like three lines, sorry paragraphs, and our bios

SIMONE: which don't mention having ever written a play.

CASSI: I can't deal with this.

SIMONE: What is this day.

CASSI: I need to hide somewhere.

SIMONE: Don't hide just scream in confused joy instead.

BOTH: Aaaaaaagh!

CASSI: Let's review – in the last two days I went on a fourth date with an actual goddess, you opened *Porgy and Bess* on the West End AND we've been invited to do our play in a four-week run. Literally is this real life?

SIMONE: May I humbly suggest that we may be...smashing it.

CASSI: We've peaked. In our mid-twenties.

SIMONE: Universe please do not strike us down.

BOTH: Let us use these opportunities wisely and deliver us from misguided artistic choices. *(Sung in harmony with the music.) Amen.*

CASSI: YES. *(Beat.)* Is this what success feels like? Just the constant sense of dread that everything is going to implode and the whole world will realise that you're a sham.

SIMONE: I mean apparently the world has turned upside down / so let's just ride the wave.

CASSI: *'The law is inside out, the world is upside down'*

SIMONE: It's mental but also congratufuckingwelldone to us.

CASSI: *'The world turned upside down down down down. / Freedom for America! Freedom –'*

SIMONE: Cass, Cass, Cass I know you're struggling to process but we're in the middle of the cafe with a finite amount of time to redraft this play, this is not the time for a musical theatre mash-up.

CASSI: Yeah but this is the other thing I don't get – it was legitimately quite shit wasn't it? Like how on earth have we even booked this slot? Clearly there was a last-minute cancellation and we just happened to tick the right boxes.

SIMONE: Or we could stop assuming that everyone has an agenda and believe that it was, in places, almost…good?

CASSI: Nah.

SIMONE: Yeah, fair. So, how do you think it went?

CASSI: Well can we talk about the fact that they just fundamentally misunderstood what we were trying to do?

SIMONE: We can. And I think it might be because we fundamentally misunderstood what we were trying to do. Or I did.

CASSI: What were you trying to do?

SIMONE: I don't know. Solve…something. Make someone feel better. That person may or may not have been me. But the songs were fun! Do you want a tea?

CASSI: Will it make me a better writer?

SIMONE: Maybe – they do cost like a tenner here now so they've probably got a little sumthin' sumthin'.

CASSI: We're actually going to have to fix it aren't we?

SIMONE: Fix, set fire to, take the money and run – three sides of the same coin, really.

CASSI: Simone.

It sinks in. It's not good.

SIMONE: Okay, look, we can do this. And preferably before the new series of *How to Get Away With Murder* comes out.

CASSI: I definitely had no idea that was happening.

SIMONE: Rewrite this play and then it's Viola and murders and meta and craploads of slow-motion eyelash removal –

BOTH: – and, 'Why. Is your penis. On a dead girl's phone?'

They realise they're being noisy.

CASSI: Lol. Good. Yes. We'll submit this new draft and then get back to normal life.

SIMONE: Yes. I'm going to go and get ma tea.

SIMONE goes and CASSI's phone pings. She scrolls.

PERSON: Hey is this seat taken?

CASSI: Yeah sorry my friend is just getting a drink.

PERSON: I really love your hair by the way.

CASSI: Thanks.

PERSON: You're actually gorgeous do you know that /
   Whereabouts are you from?

CASSI: Thanks but I'm here with my friend so – South London.

PERSON: Ah you know what I mean, where are you *from* from?

CASSI: I was born here and so were my parents. My dad's
   parents are from Ghana and my mum's Grenada.

PERSON: Nice. Well I came in for an espresso, but maybe I'll
   leave with a double mocha latte huh?

CASSI: They actually do a really great latte here.

PERSON: Or maybe a hot chocolate *(Sits down next to CASSI.)* /
   I dunno, or maybe you're more a rich cocoa slice of dark
   chocolate cake.

CASSI: Actually my friend's sitting there I just /

PERSON sings.

PERSON:

> *Chocolate woman be my roasted chestnut queen*
> *Sure I've seen those almond eyes on my laptop screen*

CASSI: Wow…

PERSON:

> *I've got a taste for strange fruit*
> *And I like it sweet and dark*
> *Black body grinding on chalk sheets*
> *Will you let me leave a mark*
>
> *On your cocoa-scented skin?*
> *On those sizzlin' mocha pins?*
> *Oh, let me take a toke on them tan twins*
> *Or I'll smash that chiselled jaw*

Avo on Brown with HP sauce. Cheers.

I'm not one you wanna ignore
'Cause I've sampled lots of spice before
I'll show you I can handle yours

Pull your courgette-spiralled hair
Suck your chocolate fingers
Taste your fleshy swollen lips
I know you want my tongue to linger
Just a trip, tantalisingly sweet, that inspires
The seed of erotic exotic desires:

Banana split 'tween your jerk chicken thighs
Smear my cream on your breasts
Like a chocolate mud pie
Spoon that fat peachy ass 'til the juices are flowin'
Start the next day with a hot espresso, and –

SIMONE: Hi, um – is everything okay?

PERSON:
I know you're dying to taste my meat
Pussy dripping 'til you slide off that café seat

SIMONE: Oh, WOW.

PERSON:
Gonna oil you down and fork that butt
Buns bouncing 'round my face, I know you like that, mutt

Don't need to order, I take what I want
You know you're my favourite restaurant

Pass the Dutchie, stir the white meat in
You know proud sour bitches get pounded up and beaten

If you want me to taste you, that smile you should sweeten
I'll whip you off the counter
Spread you out on the floor
Just a sip of my milk and you'll be begging for more

Brown sugar caramel-d bodies entwine
Digging in deep with my marble-hard tine

You got me screaming let me in!

Never seen a bitch so succulent
Squeeze those cocoa nips while I suck your c–

SIMONE: Excuse me, I think we'd like it if you actually…
went…now, please? / We've got some things to be getting
on with. Shall we just go? Let's go.

PERSON:

Imma lick you out!
Flip you up and cum inside
Nah, on your face
And then at last it'll look like mine

Music abruptly stops.

Then I'll leave another load in that big black ass…

CASSI and SIMONE leave.

PERSON: …You can't walk away from me, it's not dark enough
for you to hide. I can smell the sex on you, you spiced-rum
whore. I'll fuck you with bleach until you – until you turn
white and then take you home to my mother. Go on then
run, I don't fuck ungrateful hoes anyway – why do you
have to ruin everything, you black bitch?!

Silence. For a while.

SIMONE: Are you okay?

CASSI: …

SIMONE: Obviously you're not okay, I'm sorry. I'm really sorry that happened.

CASSI: Why are you apologising?

SIMONE: We should report it.

CASSI: Like my online stalkers.

SIMONE: Yes. Do you think he was one of them?!

CASSI: No, I think he was a dick.

More silence.

SIMONE: Well, at least we know what the problem with the play is.

CASSI: Enlighten me.

SIMONE: *'Everyone's a little bit racist… sometimes'*

CASSI: It's funny 'cause the next line is 'doesn't mean they go around committing hate crimes' but yeah…

SIMONE: …

CASSI: I just don't understand / what I did to make them think –

SIMONE: I know, / it doesn't make any sense –

CASSI: Why didn't I say something?

SIMONE: Oh.

CASSI: We've spent the last like two months writing this
show, parading about pretending to be woke, and then
something like – like this – happens and…

SIMONE: –

CASSI: We didn't – / we just let it happen.

SIMONE: It's so hard. It's one thing talking about these things
and then it happens and –

CASSI: We just do nothing?

SIMONE: Nobody did anything. Like, there were other people
there too.

CASSI: Exactly, and everyone just stood there. Did they think
it was funny or something?

SIMONE: I'm sorry.

CASSI: Why do you keep apologising? Roll on up to the
misogynoir circus, the drinks are pricey but being treated
like shit is free.

Silence. She cries. For a while. Silence.

SIMONE: Why don't we have a go at some rewrites? Maybe!
Or not? We can just –

Music begins, an opening drumbeat grows from nothing.

CASSI: Why are we even doing this. Pretending that this
will change things or make us feel better or help anyone
understand or care about anything. No matter what we
do, or what we say, all they're going to see is two 'Black
Women' on stage. They'll say it's just a story. That racism
only happens in America. If I was more smiley, less
colourful, more open, less opinionated, more agreeable,
less passionate. Maybe I wouldn't attract the wrong sort of
attention. Maybe people would feel like they could help

me. The world is not at fault. It's Black Women. It's me. I am the problem. And I deserve every bad thing that's ever happened to me because how dare I have the audacity to even draw attention to the fact that I exist. We might as well put on fucking white gloves and sing minstrel tunes and see if anyone even bats an eyelid.

SIMONE: Is that fair on them?

CASSI: I don't give a shit about fair.

SIMONE: Are we here to test them?

CASSI: Shame them. Wake them the fuck up.

SIMONE: I don't know.

I know I should have said something to that guy.

CASSI: Fuck the guy. Let's move on.

THREE

They are together, writing furiously. Until – a lightbulb moment.

CASSI: So I'm researching minstrel songs and mate I don't think I can sing any of this shit. Just found a recording of 'The Whistling Coon' which tells us of a black man who got hit in the mouth with a brick and now he can't whistle – break for laughter – everybody whistle his tune for him instead woooo.

They write furiously. Until – a lightbulb moment.

Dance from the opening.

They write furiously. Until – a lightbulb moment.

CASSI: We could call it… *The Next Black Thing*? Or *Don't Black Down*? Or *One Step Forward, Two Steps Black*?

SIMONE laughs, inconsolably.

CASSI: Or *Coloured Paper*!

Beat.

CASSI: Okay, no.

They write furiously. Until – a lightbulb moment.

They rehearse the 'Microaggression of the Week' sequence.

They write furiously. Until – a lightbulb moment.

SIMONE: *White Gloves*?

CASSI: Maybe we should steer clear of race puns?

SIMONE: It's not really a race pun, though, is it? 'Cause it's about gloves.

CASSI: I dunno, there's something that feels wrong about centring whiteness in the title, even if they are gloves.

SIMONE: *Black Gloves*?

CASSI: No gloves.

SIMONE: Was that a suggestion or a no to gloves?

They write furiously. Until – a lightbulb moment.

SIMONE: So I was reading this study and apparently a significant proportion of middle-class people self-identify as working-class but say that they only feel comfortable in middle-class settings doing middle-class things and really should be considered middle-class but, wait for it, society pigeon holes them as working-class. What class were you brought up in?

CASSI: 9C.

SIMONE: FFS.

They write furiously. Until – a lightbulb moment.

SIMONE goes to the piano and plays Bernstein's 'What's The Use'.

They write furiously. Until – a lightbulb moment.

CASSI: And I don't want to seem difficult. So I'm wearing it. This dusty yellow wig cap. A hideous gauze over my brown skin and black hair. And I want to tear it off. But there's nothing I can do. And I try to act like I don't care. But honestly it's just fucking mortifying. I ask the company manager to order me new ones. He starts laughing. And I know it's just a wig cap. But am I being stupid if I say that it feels like it means so much more?

SIMONE: And I know it's just a fact of life. But am I being stupid if I say that it feels like it means so much more?

VOICES: And I know it's just my accent / and I know it's meant to be a compliment / and I know it doesn't cost *that* much / and I know it's just his type / and I know it doesn't matter where I grew up / and I know I should have told him to stop / but it does matter, because where will we live if I don't get that paycheck / and I know it was just water but I thought it was acid and I was so scared / and I know I shouldn't feel scared / and I know I shouldn't feel so exhausted / and I know I should be able to say something / and I know it could have been worse, it could have been so much worse / I'm still here / but am I being stupid if I say that it feels like it means so much more?

They write furiously. Until – a lightbulb moment.

SIMONE: How about something in-your-face and provocative? *Every N-Word is a Star*?

CASSI: We *can't* use that.

SIMONE: I suppose it would be weird to pick a title we can't say aloud.

CASSI: *Shuck 'n' Jive.*

A pause. They take it in.

SIMONE: I like it.

CASSI: Sounds like the name of a chicken shop.

They write furiously. Until – their phones ring.

FOUR

They check their phones. SIMONE answers on loudspeaker.

PRODUCER: Ladies, hi, so we've had a few notes in.

SIMONE and CASSI look to each other in confusion.

PRODUCER: So, it's quite embarrassing really, but our literary
department thinks it's lacking diversity.

CASSI: What do you mean?

SIMONE: Diver–

PRODUCER: So obviously we have both of you, which is, by
the way, great, brilliant, wonderful, mmmh? But we all
know that just casting diversely isn't enough. We need to
truly interrogate the stories we are telling as well as who is
telling them.

SIMONE: Yeah, definitely –

PRODUCER: I'm glad you agree. So you've got all this
very compelling material about life as a black woman
and how you're 'not a monolith', but are you capable
of communicating that to the audience? We've got this
amazing young man on our books at the moment, very
experienced writer, he could really make something of
what you've got so far.

SIMONE: A writ–

PRODUCER: Transform it into a truly human story – less of that charmingly predictable woe-is-me-life-is-so-hard-because-someone-touched-my-hair narrative. He'll write something about people being people. It's a bit much at the moment, with all the Beyoncé, and it's not a show about slavery but also it's not terribly accessible, is it?

CASSI: I'm sorry but – 'it's a bit much'?

SIMONE: I actually agree with her on that one. I think it needs to be a story that is intrinsically human about normal people which happens to have societal inequality as a backdrop. So it's accessible enough to maybe actually effect some change.

PRODUCER: Great, brilliant, one second girls. KP, I need you to proof –

PRODUCER puts them on hold.

CASSI: What was that?

SIMONE: Was what?

CASSI: She said our play wasn't about normal people and you agreed with her.

SIMONE: I… I'm sorry. I didn't mean to agree with her. Shit, did I just agree with her? I think I just blacked out…

CASSI: And accidentally agreed to have the whole thing rewritten by a white man?

SIMONE: She didn't say he was white.

CASSI: We both know that if he was anything other than white she would have mentioned it.

SIMONE: Shiiii–

PRODUCER is back on the line.

PRODUCER: So great news, he's said yes to the project and can get to work on the new version ASAP.

SIMONE: Oh we were just wondering whether maybe you could run us through what you had in mind / before we agreed to anything for certain?

CASSI: *Actually* we were just saying that we've put a lot of ourselves into this project and I'm worried that this *ghostwriter* won't understand our perspective –

PRODUCER: Well which one is it? Do you want his help or do you want to do this all on your own?

CASSI: I just want to make sure that our content isn't diluted so you have something more commercially viable –

SIMONE: What Cass means is we're really grateful for your support but it would be great to maybe meet the / ghostwriter first.

PRODUCER: Honestly ladies, listen to yourselves, you're clearly not on the same page, and that's really no way to make theatre. This is precisely why the end goal is for him to take over as your new writer – you'll still be in it, of course. Look at that – a whole show, written just for you, that's what you wanted, wasn't it?

SIMONE: No!

CASSI: You said you wanted this play, our play. Not just something with our faces in it.

PRODUCER: If you want to write for yourselves, keep a diary. You can trust him, he'll create something everybody can understand.

CASSI: Look we're literally working on another draft right now. I can't promise you that everybody will relate to it, but could you at least give us a chance to do this our way before you hand everything / over to –

PRODUCER: Ladies there's really no shame in asking for help – KP, what was that? – Girls, I'm excited about this new direction. I thought you were too. Either you hand over to the new writer now or send me another draft, but if I don't like it then that's the end of the road. We'll go our separate ways. I don't want it to come to that, but honestly I don't have time for all this umm-ing and ahh-ing, mmh.

PRODUCER hangs up.

FIVE

They resume writing, now in separate locations, on Google Docs.

SIMONE: Waiting for an Uber with thirty kilos of pebbles, a wheelie bed and a packet of chips.

Uber app pings.

CASSI: Train to Aberdeen, hour four.

Train tracks.

SIMONE: How long left now?

CASSI: Train or tour?

SIMONE: Surprise me.

CASSI: Roughly seven weeks, four days, six hours and thirty-two minutes.

SIMONE: On the *train?*

CASSI: The joke was in the 'roughly'.

SIMONE: I'm not here to punch your lines for you.

CASSI: I'll punch your lights out in a minute.

SIMONE: I can do Thursday evening?

CASSI: I'll be lipsing my girlfriend.

SIMONE: Mmmm, okay. What's her deal?

CASSI: *'I like big butts and I cannot lie'*

SIMONE: Damn straight.

CASSI: Let's link up afternoon near Guy's Hospital?

SIMONE: I have class and they'll Jeremy Hunt me down if
I'm late.

CASSI: *(Guffaws.)* Where you headed to now baby girl?

SIMONE: I's gone props sourcing and tryna get back fo' the
next rehearsal but no dice.

CASSI: Oh –

SIMONE: No cigar?

CASSI: Close but –

SIMONE: No banana.

CASSI snaps in a Z shape.

> I'm hoping they'll expense this but what if they don't and
> I've waited and miss the rehearsal and then they won't
> pay me for that either. Imma walk.

CASSI: Bye Felicia.

SIMONE: Peace out muthafucka.

Uber dings stop. Brief pause.

SIMONE: All the wheels fell off the bed.

CASSI: *(Guffaws.)* Deadddd.

SIMONE: This bed cost the same as my pay for the week and they're only using it in one rehear–

How 'bout ten on Thursday? Going once, going twice…

CASSI: Why we gots ta do Thursday anyway?

SIMONE: I was thinking we should take up cotton pickin'. Or we could just do coffee, I don't mind.

CASSI: And I knows you're more of a tea person so that's punishment enough.

SIMONE: What am I being punished for again?

CASSI: I ask myself that every day.

SIMONE: Dark.

CASSI: For bare shit jokes.

SIMONE: Yeah, my baby daddy went down for that – I got away with community service – that's why…I'm…hanging out…with you.

CASSI kisses teeth.

SIMONE: I can't even pretend – I love you, boo, I would say next week but we ain't gon' get our timetable 'til Friyay because school might as well be run by BoJo's barber.

CASSI: Nah blud that just ain't it. How you meant to do important shit like get your weave did if mans won't tell you when you're needed?

SIMONE: Me nuh no gyal… Did I tell you I got confused for the other lightie at school three times this week?

CASSI: The audacity of the caucacity! I's was talm bout whens I done taken some time off school an dis cracker chick tells er'ry damn sucka that I's been kicked out for dealing.

SIMONE: Allow that, those pussies are bare moist, fam. Taxi's here, thank the sweet lawd for that, think I'm hypervent–

CASSI: BLACKFACE AT THE MET –

SIMONE: – IN 2019 –

CASSI: – IN 2k19!

SIMONE: – and then they wonder why only yt pipo do opera, and dem aristocratic muthafuckas.

CASSI: Simone, man cannot live on bread alone. But you know what he can live on? Puccini. Puccini is food enough for the summer. Or just don't eat and call it character research for *La Bohème*.

RECEPTIONIST: Hey girl hey, welcome to Stroud Green Food Bank. Oh golly you look awful! Can I take your name and we'll get you a food packet right away you poor little pickaninny?

SIMONE: '*Sì. Mi chiamano Mimì ma il mio nome è Lucia…*'

RECEPTIONIST: Excuse me – excuse me! Can somebo– EXCUSE ME, CAN YOU PLEASE –

They stop writing.

SIMONE: AH.

CASSI: Sorry, what?

SIMONE: …

Do you really think I'd say 'they'll Jeremy Hunt me down if I'm late'?

CASSI: That's the only line you have an issue with?

SIMONE: Take one spoon of obscure highbrow cutaway, add a dash of poverty, roll with LGBTQ representation,

fry it all in 'urban slang', and you've got a performative
wokeness festival.

CASSI: *(Laughs.)* Well, we tried. We lol'ed. We failed. Can we
go back to writing what's true now?

SIMONE: Yeah, let's lay this draft to rest. Rice 'n' peas. Urgh,
it's catching.

They delete the scene.

SIX

They continue to write, still in separate locations, on Google Docs.

SIMONE: Waiting for an Uber with thirty kilos of pebbles, a
wheelie bed and a packet of chips.

CASSI: When am I going to see you?

SIMONE: Can we pencil in Thursday? But I can't confirm
yet as we won't get our timetable for next week 'til Friday
because school is an arse.

CASSI: Why are they like this?

SIMONE: I don't think it's malicious, just – life is…hard,
ya know. / For everyo–

CASSI: But how are you meant to do important things like
see your friends and I dunno actually book in work so
you can pay your course fees if they won't tell you when
you're needed?

SIMONE: Cass didn't you hear? Only rich people can do
art now.

CASSI: Are you rich?

SIMONE: Well, no.

CASSI: So non-rich people can do art.

SIMONE: Well maybe I am rich.

> I just took a taxi but it was from an unbranded chicken shop and I went to an opera rehearsal and I was the Assistant Director but I was doing manual labour and on my way home I'll go to M&S cause it's the only thing that will be open that late after work and my local is a Waitrose but it's cheaper to live there than by the Lidl and I buy fresh fruit every day and I'm so lost and – and I've never eaten steak and I got music lessons as a child but I can't afford to earn money from it as an adult and I cut my hair biennially but I use the word biennially and I can't pronounce it right and I might get kicked out of school for doing work but if I don't do work I might get kicked out of school and they say I sound down to earth and you should speak in RP and I don't know what my accent isn't and can you be a working-class vegan and are you even a vegan anyway if you got your chips from a chicken shop and I'm half-white but I'm whole black and somehow that makes me less than one person and maybe that's why I can't do maths and why I can't do money and why I can't *do* and now all the wheels have fallen off my bed and I'm clutching my pebble and talking to myself and somebody just thought I was homeless and they spit shame and I get paid weekly and I rent a flat and yesterday I played croquet –

Blackout.

SEVEN

CASSI: Shimone…

SIMONE:

CASSI: Simone. Are you alright?

SIMONE:

CASSI: Are you okay?

SIMONE: Yeah. Yeah. Yeah.

CASSI: Three yeah's. Methinks the lady doth protest too much.

SIMONE: It's actually 'the lady doth protest too much, methinks'.

CASSI: I was trying to be nice to you.

SIMONE: Don't do that.

CASSI: Don't be nice?

SIMONE: Yeah, be nice. Please.

CASSI: …

SIMONE: Say something nice. Please.

CASSI: Erm. Penguins mate for life? Oh wait did you mean… to you.

SIMONE: No, that was nice, I liked that.

CASSI: Oh. Okay. Good.

SIMONE: …

CASSI: Well, I'm also going to say something nice to you.

SIMONE: Penguins are cute.

CASSI: Honestly if I woke up tomorrow and had to choose between forty-seven unread messages from you or a single notification telling me that you'd left the country forever then I'd absolutely pick the former. And that's really saying something because you know I hate when people send a million sentence-length messages rather than just using paragraphs.

SIMONE: Th-thank you. *(Breathes.)*

CASSI listens.

But you literally always send me loads of individual sentences.

CASSI: And my awesome capacity for cognitive dissonance is what makes me a brilliant artist.

SIMONE: …

CASSI: I miss you.

SIMONE: We text each other every day.

CASSI: Yeah but I miss your face, and your company, and…

SIMONE: What's happening?

CASSI: What do you mean what's happening?

SIMONE: I don't know. I just. Didn't expect. This. I'm sorry you miss me.

CASSI: Stop apologising, we're nearly at the end of the play, you're supposed to have learnt something, at least let it be that you don't have to apologise for everything.

SIMONE: No, no, I don't think that's my takeaway from this – wait, I don't think we're supposed to be writing the play in this scene.

CASSI: Yeah, of course we are – … No, you're right, we're not.

SIMONE: I don't know what's real anymore.

CASSI: Neither do I.

BOTH: …

CASSI: When was the last time we spoke about real things? Like actual real-life things rather than this pseudo-utopia we've concocted for ourselves where we get to relive our trauma over and over again and call it entertainment?

SIMONE: I mean, do we have to?

CASSI: Talk about real things?

SIMONE: No, I mean, I'm not sure we should. Write the play.

CASSI: I'm so confused.

SIMONE: I was thinking about what happened. And how I thought we should have said something to that guy. But we shouldn't have said something, we should have done something.

CASSI: How does this relate to the play? Where has all this come from?

SIMONE: I'm on my period. But I'm not emotional, I'm just honest. Have we written all this stuff just to come to the conclusion that, you know, people think we're black? We are black, I mean, people think we're what they think of as 'Black' – 'Hi, I'm Simone, I turn up three hours late to gospel choir with some fried chicken in hand, saying "mmm, mmm-hmm", clicking my fingers even though my hands are full of fried chicken – it's just something we can do.' We could have *said* that in three seconds, I just did.

CASSI: Yeah, but it's not as good.

SIMONE: No, it's not. It's not as good as *doing* something. As spending the however much time we've spent writing this going to the Stroud Green Food Bank eleven a.m. to one p.m. every other Saturday and sorting the dry goods into order by use by so that we don't give away all the newest stuff –

CASSI: That's weirdly specific.

SIMONE: You're weirdly specific.

CASSI: Like, have you actually done that?

SIMONE: No, I haven't, because I've been here.

CASSI: Not every other Saturday morning.

SIMONE: Metaphorically. I've spent those Saturday mornings that I could have been doing something, anything, useful for the world, thinking about art, okay watching Netflix, but watching Netflix and thinking about art and representation in that art and how great it is that a young black girl might watch *How to Get Away With Murder* and think 'one day that could be me', and then having a state-of-the-nation conversation with my housemate before signing a quick petition and sitting down to write more of this. When was the last time I actually volunteered for that food bank? Or went on one of those marches? Or even just read a newspaper?

CASSI: I don't know, when was the last time you read a newspaper? So what are you saying then – you want to stop writing the play?

SIMONE: …

CASSI: Is this because of the ghostwriter thing? Because I think it's ridiculous that she'd genuinely rather cancel the play than let us / write it ourselves.

SIMONE: Cass… Do you think that maybe she could be right though? It's taken up so much time already and we're still struggling to – I dunno… But I do know there's no point in writing a lecture, no matter how much singing and dancing there is. We're just people talking to other people and we need to put people things on stage. Get off our high horses…or…take a step back and accept that someone else could write it better.

CASSI: No.

We have to finish what we started
You got us half-way there
This wasn't my idea – remember?
But now you're running scared.

You're always so quick to lighten the tone and
Apologise for your existence
Proximity to whiteness is your key to self-subsistence

SIMONE:

'Proximity to whiteness is my key' –
How can you even say that to me? We
Both 'lighten the tone' as a way to survive
Or have you forgotten this is shuck 'n' jive?

I just don't understand
Why else you'd suggest that
We should be replaced.
Your way of surviving is futile
If our voices get displaced

I don't see what's so wrong
With letting someone help us
The play will still be on
*And **he***

He will whiten the perspective

Could widen our perspective

And ignore the collective
Weight *of*

Wait.

*our **trauma***

You're not *listening.*
Our creation it's *– done what?*

Our creation it's *like –*
it isn't a fanciful fabrication

What, then?

And I will not go back
To singing slave songs on a fictional plantation
Because somehow that's more plausible
More accessible than watching me:
A woman born in 1993
Struggle.

I'm asking about the people who live that life now –

'No that's a lie.

What?

We've solved diversity –

How?

With all those sistas on the West End.
singing about the Swanee.'

Fuck me

While I cry a river of tears

We're saying the same thing
All we both want is to do something
Better than
Pretending

Because

Because *in reality*

Every hoe

                            *I just **don't know***

*And **crack whore***

                           *Who this **is for.***

And ghetto queen
Teach the masses, like that guy, that once I hit sixteen
From the chrysalis bursts a sassy sex-machine
Because that's all they've been
Conditioned to see

                           Apart from you

They're blind to the ravine between
Me

                           *and **me***
                           Railing against.

and

what the media would have us be

What made you believe you have to choose
Between making art and fighting poverty?
Bet Olivier never faced this dichotomy
Man just stood, and spoke, and soaked up the applause,
Blackened his face in pursuit of more –

                           Olivier wasn't poor.

SIMONE: I do have to choose between making art and fighting poverty. Most people do.

CASSI: I hear that, but still… shouldn't *everyone* be able to use art to change their situation?

SIMONE:
*Can't you see **there's more***

CASSI:
*And I know **there's more***

More to life than make-up and lights
More than white men posturing in brown tights

But we can't let them tell us
This was all a waste of time

Was this all a waste of time?

Because this is our space too

We tried to make this space to
escape
A

Our

little corner of the world

where we can do

Where we could do

Something

*And it's absolutely **worthwhile***

*And is it **worthwhile***

Even if that something is only
To persuade others that they can do

Something too

Something too?

This is our corner of the universe
And we will stand and be seen

We will speak and be heard
And I will clap and cry **and**

          And *should I*

      shout and sing and
        laugh and
       transform...

           While others

Unburdened of the tropes that shackled me

      Are burdened by the tropes that shackled me

Because this

         Even though *this waste of time*
         Is literally **the first time**

This is **the first time**

       I've felt free.

SIMONE: So we carry on?

CASSI: Yeah.

Beat. The crushing moment of realisation. It consumes them.

CASSI: And that's the play.

It is. The theatrical world begins its wind-down process.

SIMONE: I hate to interrupt but that's a shit ending.

The theatrical world pauses, or this becomes a race to finish the conversation before the fade-out engulfs them.

SIMONE: Wouldn't it be more radical just to write something
    joyful? How often do we get to see that – people like us
    just being happy? People like us just – being.

This is the way the play ends – not with a bang but with the whisper of a new beginning. As they breathe in the silence, music fades in, and their breaths begin to move in time.

EIGHT

OLIVIA: Hello.

TANISHA: Heya.

OLIVIA: Hi.

…

I'm *(go right ahead and insert your name and a thing about yourself here).*

TANISHA: I'm *(and now you).*

BOTH: We have just met.

They begin to dance again. It is different to before and perhaps more beautiful now. Their hands are beginning to burn and they don't know why.

We love music.

…

And we love the theatre:

TANISHA: its power to move

OLIVIA: and to teach

TANISHA: to change a mind,

OLIVIA: open a heart,

TANISHA: eye,

OLIVIA: mouth,

TANISHA: pocket,

OLIVIA: to communicate

TANISHA: live*

OLIVIA: something to a group of people who may never have met each other,

TANISHA: sat next to each other,

OLIVIA: treat** each other like human beings with minds and feelings just like them –

TANISHA: another qualia-soaked, newly behoped –

OLIVIA: by something dope

TANISHA: like theatre

OLIVIA: or music;

TANISHA: if it hadn't been for theatre

OLIVIA: or iPlayer

TANISHA: or Netflix

OLIVIA: or music

TANISHA: or something that doesn't have a name

OLIVIA: yet

BOTH: like this

    ...

but that soon will.

TANISHA: Something that tries its best / to

---

*   *adverb – pronunciation should rhyme with 'jive'*
** *past tense – pronunciation should rhyme with 'met'*

OLIVIA: to put something good and / to

TANISHA: to put something fun and / to

OLIVIA: to put something true / into

TANISHA: into the world.

TANISHA and OLIVIA take each other by one wrist and peel back the skin of their hands. Pain relief. Oh, it was only a flesh-coloured glove, now inside out. The inside is bright white. They toss the gloves away. They do the same with their other hands. They see each other. They ready themselves for the next story.

NINE

Music is playing.

The audience leave.

END

WWW.OBERONBOOKS.COM

Printed in the USA
CPSIA information can be obtained
at www.ICGtesting.com
LVHW020958171024
794056LV00004B/1219